ONE STEP AT A TIME

By Howard Gutner
Illustrated by Jane Kendall

Modern Curriculum Press
Parsippany, New Jersey

Ashlin's book

Modern
Curriculum
Press

Pearson Learning Group

1-800-321-3106
www.pearsonlearning.com

CONTENTS

To all the brave men, women, and children who traveled west to find a new way of life

CHAPTER 1

THE WAY WEST

"Whoa!" Joe Carter called as he pulled up on the reins. The four oxen pulling his wagon halted. Behind him, 20 other wagons slowly came to a stop, one after the other.

Joe jumped down from the wagon. He walked down the line of wagons and pointed to a group of trees some distance away. "We'll stop for the night here!" he shouted. "There's shade and grass for the animals, and water beyond those trees."

Sarah Harding and her mother stopped alongside their wagon and began to shake the dust from their skirts. "I've never seen so much dust in all my life," Mrs. Harding said.

Mr. Harding jumped down from the wagon and walked over to Sarah. "Please go find your brother," he said. "You two need to take the buckets and get some water for the animals."

"I'm so tired," Sarah whined. "I just want to sit down."

"Not yet," Mrs. Harding said. "We're all tired, but there's work to be done before resting."

Sarah sighed and walked around the wagon. "JACK!" she yelled. Her brother came running.

"Father says we have to get some water for the animals," Sarah told him.

"All right," said Jack as he unhooked two leather buckets from the side of the wagon. He handed one to Sarah.

"Can't you carry it?" Sarah said.

"No," Jack said, "I can't do your work and mine, too." Sarah reluctantly took her bucket and followed him to the stream.

"Come on, Scout," Jack called as they walked. A black-and-white dog bounded to his side. "I don't think you ever get tired," Jack said as he smiled at his dog. "We must have walked 20 miles today, and you're still ready to go."

"Jack," Sarah said as they walked to the stream, "why are we doing this?"

"Doing what?" Jack asked.

"You know, leaving Missouri to go to the Oregon Territory," she said.

"It's a little late to be worrying about that now," Jack replied. "Papa said our farm back east wasn't making any money. He heard there was free land in the Oregon Territory, land so rich the crops almost grow by themselves."

As he talked, Jack remembered the night his mother and father had been worrying about money. His father said the neighbors had received a letter from friends who had gone to the Oregon Territory last year, in 1843. They wrote about a beautiful land with mild winters. Jack's mother finally agreed to go, and they had started out in April. Now it was June and they had traveled nearly 700 miles along the Oregon Trail in a wagon train.

"The farm is sold and gone," Jack said, "so we can't turn back now."

"I'm tired of getting up so early every morning and walking all day," Sarah complained.

Jack laughed. "That's how you get somewhere, Sarah; one step at a time!"

As Jack and Sarah started back to the wagons, they heard a shout. They turned as Scout barked and wagged his tail. Their friend Ben Hamilton was trying to catch up to them, carrying his own bucket filled with water.

Seeing Ben always made Sarah smile. The
Hamiltons were from the east, too. They had
come all the way from Philadelphia. To Sarah,
Ben still looked like he had just come from the
city because he always wore a cap and a white
shirt that was as clean as possible, no matter how
hot the weather.

"Sarah is getting impatient, Ben," Jack
chuckled. "She wants to get to the Oregon
Territory tomorrow or go back to Missouri!"

Ben put down his bucket and began looking through his pockets.

"What are you looking for?" Sarah asked.

"The map that my father and I made," Ben replied. He pulled out a wrinkled piece of paper and spread it on the ground.

"Here, Sarah, look. Tomorrow we should get to the place where we cross the North Platte River. After that, it's only a little over a hundred miles to South Pass. Then we're halfway there."

"Just halfway?" Sarah cried. "We'll never make it. My feet will be worn out by then."

NIGHT ON THE PRAIRIE

When Jack, Sarah, and Ben returned, the wagons had already been pulled into a circle. The oxen and other animals were tied to the wagons inside the circle. The children gave water to the animals, and the women looked for firewood. Every day they found less wood to use for cooking fires. Some of the women gathered dried buffalo droppings they called chips. Joe Carter had reassured them the chips would burn well.

Sarah helped her mother peel a few potatoes before supper. Mrs. Harding put two large kettles on the fire, one with beans and the other with the potatoes and some beef bones left over from the night before. As Jack peeked into one of the pots, his father, who was sitting nearby, smiled at him.

"We might have to go hunting tomorrow or the next day, son," Mr. Harding said.

Jack turned to Scout. "Hear that, Scout? You want to help me catch some rabbits?" Scout barked. He was always ready to go.

"Evening, folks!" Joe Carter said as he walked into the light of the fire. "I just wanted to tell you that tomorrow we'll be getting up before sunrise again. I want to try to get across the North Platte River before dark."

There were some groans from the other wagons. "I know, folks, I know," Joe said, "but we've got to get past the mountains before the snow starts to fall, or we'll be in sad shape. It'll take us the whole day to get across the river."

After dinner the camp settled down for the
night. Everyone was too tired to play the fiddle or
sing. No one even talked much. Jack, Sarah, and
Ben laid their blankets outside near the fire. They
were still talking after the adults were asleep.

"What was it like living in Philadelphia, Ben?"
Sarah whispered.

"You're always asking me that," Ben said.

"I've never been to a big city," Sarah said.

"Well," said Ben, "mostly I remember the shops, wonderful shops where you could buy anything, like candles, clothes, and bread. There were lots of carriages and people on the street. Philadelphia was never silent like this."

All three of them were quiet for a moment, listening. All they could hear in the darkness were the small movements of the oxen and a creak from a wagon. Suddenly Scout whined.

"What is it, boy?" Jack asked. A moment passed; then they heard a mournful howl.

"What is that?" Ben gasped.

"It's a wolf," Jack whispered. Sarah and Ben's eyes widened with fear. "It sounds far away, but don't worry. Wolves almost never attack people."

The howl sounded again. This time it was answered by another howl. Scout began to growl softly. "It's all right, boy!" Jack patted him on the head. "They won't come near the camp." Jack felt as frightened as Sarah and Ben looked. He began to feel a little sorry for his sister. She was a pest, but she was just a child. They were all so far away from everything they knew.

Jack laid back and looked up at the night sky, dotted with twinkling stars. "Should we sleep in the wagon?" Sarah whispered. She was still worried about the wolves.

"We'll be all right. Scout will warn us if there's any real danger," Jack said. To himself, he added, "I hope."

CHAPTER 3

RIVER CROSSING

It was still dark the next morning when Jack, Sarah, and Ben woke up to the delicious smell of sizzling bacon.

"Hurry and get some breakfast, children," Mrs. Harding said.

The three jumped up to get their plates of bacon with fresh biscuits. Jack laughed as Ben tossed pieces of bacon to Scout, who leaped in the air to catch them.

"It's about ten miles to the river crossing,"
Jack's father said, as everyone cleaned up. "Jack,
I think we'd better look for some game later
today."

"Game?" asked Ben. "Why would your father
want to play a game?"

"No, no," Sarah laughed. "Game means
animals. He meant they'll go hunting so we can
have some fresh meat."

Early that afternoon the wagon train stopped beside a wide, swiftly flowing river.

"It will be a while before it's our turn to cross the river," Mr. Harding said to Jack. "I've got to talk to Joe, so you take the rifle and go with Scout to hunt for rabbits."

"Can I ask Ben to come along?" Jack asked.

"Yes, just be careful," his father said.

Jack walked over to the Hamilton's wagon and asked if Ben could come hunting with him.

"Oh, I don't know," Mrs. Hamilton said. She looked worried and glanced at her husband. "Ben has never been hunting before."

"Let him go, Martha," Mr. Hamilton said. "He's going to have to learn sometime, and he will need to know how to hunt in Oregon."

"Don't worry, Mr. Hamilton," Jack said. "I know what I'm doing, and we have Scout with us, too."

"All right," sighed Mrs. Hamilton as the two boys started walking with Scout leading the way.

"How do you find rabbits?" asked Ben, as they entered the tall grass.

"Shhh," Jack whispered. "You have to be quiet for one thing. Keep watching Scout. He knows what we're looking for."

Ben watched as Scout walked slowly through the grass ahead of them. He stopped, smelled the ground, then peered through the grass. Suddenly his ears went up.

Jack quickly put his hand on Ben's shoulder, warning him not to move. He aimed the rifle and fired. "Got it!" Jack yelled, as Scout ran to pick up the rabbit.

When the boys returned from hunting, a few
of the wagons had already crossed the river.
There was one more wagon to go before the
Hardings crossed.

Jack showed his mother the rabbit. "Good,"
Mrs. Harding said, "we can have rabbit stew
tonight. Now go and help the men with the
wagons. The Connollys had a rough time getting
across. Their wagon almost tipped over."

Just then Joe Carter rode down the line of
wagons. "The lighter the load in your wagon, the
easier it will be to get across. See what you can
leave behind!" he announced.

Jack saw his mother turn pale as Joe rode by. "Do you think we need to lighten our load, John?" she asked her husband.

Mr. Harding sighed, "It wouldn't hurt, Margaret. Let's see what we can spare."

After a while, Mr. Harding called Jack into the wagon. Together they carried out a wooden dresser and set it on the ground. Mrs. Harding looked close to tears, but her husband said he would make her another dresser when they got to Oregon. Jack looked down the line of wagons and saw a piano, a washtub, and a large mirror all sitting on the ground.

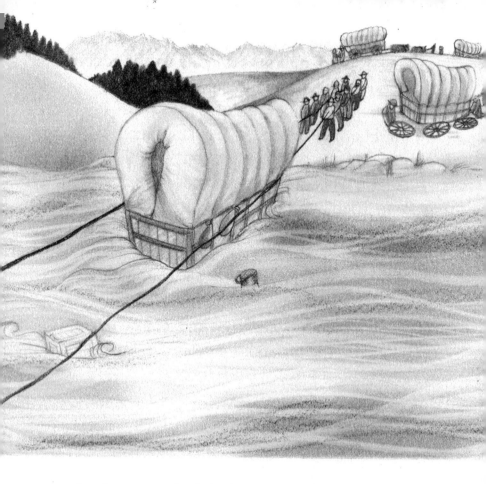

At the river, Jack helped his father take the
wheels off the wagon. Ben's father and some
men from another wagon helped Mr. Harding
stretch a rope from one side of the river to the
other. Men were already on the other side
waiting to pull the rope and guide the wagon
across. The women and children would ride in
the wagons, but the animals had to swim across.

The river looked rough. Jack asked his father if Scout could ride in the wagon.

"Dogs are good swimmers, Jack," his father said. "Scout used to swim that creek near our house back home. He'll be fine." Jack began to argue with him, but then something happened.

The ropes had snapped on a nearby wagon, and it was sinking into the river. Jack and his family could hear screams, but there was nothing anyone could do.

"Was anybody inside?" Jack shouted.

"I don't know," his father said. "We can't wait, or the ropes on our wagon might break!"

"Jack! Sarah! Hurry!" Jack looked up and saw that his mother was already in the wagon. He took Sarah's hand and hurried to join her.

The moment Jack and Sarah stepped into the wagon, they both let out a shout. There were already two inches of icy cold water in the bottom, and the river was moving so fast! They both hung on as the wagon turned sideways, then pulled straight. Jack watched anxiously as Scout swam behind the wagon.

Suddenly, when they were halfway across, the wagon started to tip, and Jack lost sight of Scout. By the time he spotted him, it was too late. Scout had drifted downriver, far from the wagon.

"Scout!" Jack shouted. "Swim, boy!"

Jack's father moved to keep the wagon from tipping over and tried to catch Scout as the water carried him by. He couldn't reach the struggling dog without falling out of the wagon.

Jack and Sarah could see Scout trying to fight the river. His paws kept splashing, but he could not keep his head up. The water carried him farther, and then, suddenly, he disappeared.

"Scout!!" Jack and Sarah screamed as their wagon kept moving steadily toward the shore.

As soon as they reached land, Jack jumped out. "We have to go back!" he shouted wildly.

"Jack, listen to me," Mr. Harding said, staring into Jack's face. "We can't go back. I feel as bad as you do, son, but the wagon train won't wait for us. We can't cross the country on our own."

"Jack," his mother said softly, "we may have lost Scout, but there's still a chance he'll swim to safety. It could have been worse." She nodded sadly toward the family near them who'd lost their wagon earlier. The parents had each dragged one of the children inside to safety. Now they huddled, wet and gasping for breath, on the riverbank.

Jack gazed up at his parents and saw the tears in their eyes. Then Jack fell down on the riverbank and began to cry. Sarah came over and put her hands on his shoulders.

"I'm sorry, Jack," she said quietly. She was crying, too. For once Jack didn't push her away, but he didn't want to talk to her. Silently he got up. He helped his father and the other men put the wheels back on their wagon, and hitch up the oxen. He kept looking across the river, but it was no use. Scout was gone.

CHAPTER 4

INDEPENDENCE ROCK

The next few days were hard for Jack. All he could think of was Scout, but he couldn't be alone with his thoughts. His family needed his help.

As the land became drier and the air became hotter, the travelers knew they were nearing the desert. They had a harder time finding fresh water, cooking fuel, and good grass for the animals. At day's end, it took longer to find the things they needed to make camp. The animals were also tiring.

In July the wagon train came to Independence Rock. From a distance the big pile of stone looked like a bear sleeping on its side. Earlier wagon trains had named it Independence Rock because they had reached it on July 4, Independence Day. That was the day people celebrated the founding of the United States.

Ben called to Jack and pointed at the huge rock, but Jack only nodded in response. He kept looking back at the trail, as if he expected Scout to come running after them.

After the wagons made camp, Ben wanted to go see the names carved in the soft rock, but Jack said he didn't feel like it. He stayed to help his father fix a wagon wheel while Ben visited the rock with Sarah.

As Mrs. Harding made breakfast the next morning, Joe Carter came up to their wagon. "Two of the Shermans' oxen died last night," he said. "I told them to throw away everything they could to make it easier on the animals they have left. You might want to look again at your wagon. We have to lighten our loads or the animals won't make it."

John Harding looked at his wife and she nodded. They went into the wagon, and a little while later Sarah saw them carrying out the chest full of Mrs. Harding's fine china.

"No, Mama, not our beautiful dishes! Can't we leave something else?" Sarah cried.

"It's the heaviest thing we have, Sarah," her father said. "The oxen are more important now."

Mrs. Harding turned and looked at Sarah. "If I had known this would happen, I would have left these things with your Aunt June," she said. Sarah rushed forward and hugged her mother.

An hour later, Sarah found Jack watering the oxen by a small creek. She was carrying a large bundle and crying.

"Do you remember when Uncle William sent these to me?" she asked her brother.

Jack turned a corner of the cloth and saw three dolls their uncle had sent Sarah for her birthday three years ago. They were made of china. Each of them had silken hair and bright blue eyes made of glass.

Jack smiled. "You really love these dolls, don't you?" he asked. Sarah looked at the ground as she handed the dolls to Jack and wiped her eyes.

"I don't play with them much anymore, but I wanted to keep them," she sobbed. "Papa says they're too heavy, and we have to leave them behind with the china."

Jack felt the dolls in his hand. They were heavy, but he knew why Sarah wanted to keep them. Uncle William had died last year, and the dolls were one of the few things Sarah had that Uncle William had given her.

Sarah touched the dolls' soft hair. "Oh, Jack," she said, "I feel as if we're giving up everything. First Scout, and now . . ." She trailed off.

Jack gave the dolls back to Sarah and put his arm around her. "We've still got our family. That's what counts," Jack said. "Look how many people have lost family members on this trip."

Sarah dried her eyes. "I guess you're right," she said. "You know what? I'm going to ask Papa if I can keep just one doll. One doll won't weigh so much, will it?"

"Of course not," Jack said. He was proud of his little sister. She was growing up fast. "Come on," he said, "I'll go with you."

When the wagons left the next day, it looked as if the Hardings were leaving a whole house behind them. Mrs. Harding had also set out her wash bowl and a wood cabinet. Other people left dishes and books, and even a desk. On top of the desk were two beautiful dolls with blue eyes.

CHAPTER 5

A FORK IN THE ROAD

In the afternoon the wagon train stopped at the Sweetwater River. After everyone was settled, Joe told a story about how the river got its name.

"About ten years ago," he said, "some trappers were passing through here. They tried to get across the river during a storm. One of their packs was full of sugar, and when it broke, about 300 pounds of sugar spilled into the river!"

Jack laughed out loud, and Sarah smiled. It was the first time Jack had laughed since that terrible day they had crossed the North Platte River.

The next day the wagon train twisted its way
through rocky hills. The sun was hot, so Sarah and
Jack walked in the shade of the wagon with their
mother. All of a sudden, Sarah jumped onto the
moving wagon and hid inside. She refused to come
out even though Jack teased her.

Jack looked around to see what could possibly
have scared her. Then he saw them. There were
rattlesnakes everywhere, coiled up in the shade of
the rocks.

"They were here long before we ever came,"
Mr. Harding said. "If you don't bother them,
they're not going to bother you. We just have to be
careful, that's all."

Finally the wagon train moved out of the hills onto a flat, rocky plain. The weather was colder, but still very dry. To the north were snow-covered mountains.

When the wagons stopped at midday, Joe announced they were traveling through the South Pass, which meant that the wagon train was halfway to the Oregon Territory. Everyone cheered, and Ben grabbed Sarah and began dancing around.

Three days after the wagon train passed by the mountains, they came to a fork where the trail divided. Joe called a meeting that night to talk about a shortcut that headed north.

"If we take the shortcut, it will save us seven days," he said, "but we'll have to go at night. This trail covers several miles of desert, and it would be too hot to travel during the day. There will be no water or grass for the animals."

Joe said he thought it would be safer to go southwest. It would take longer, but the land was not so dry or hot. They could also stop at Fort Bridger to get supplies.

John Harding thought that his family should go with Joe, and his wife agreed. "The oxen will never be able to travel that fast," she said, "and I don't want to walk at night. Besides, how will we sleep during the day, with the sun so hot?"

Sarah said she didn't want to walk at night either. Jack thought she was probably more worried about stepping on a rattlesnake in the dark than she was about sleeping in the hot sun.

Later that evening, Ben came over to Jack and Sarah's wagon. His eyes looked red and puffy, as if he'd been crying.

"We're going to take the shortcut with four other families," he said, sitting down next to the campfire. "My father wants to get to Oregon as soon as possible."

Jack looked at Ben and then turned away. "We won't be seeing you again, I guess."

"We'll see you in Oregon!" Sarah said. "Don't forget we're all going to the same place. We're just taking different trails."

"That's right," Ben said, trying to smile. "You watch out for rattlesnakes, Sarah."

Sarah shuddered. "I will, Ben."

"Jack, I'm still so sorry about Scout. I wish things could have been different. I miss him, and I'm going to miss you, too," Ben said.

Jack looked at his friend and tried to smile. He didn't want to cry. He was tired of crying.

"I'm going to miss you, too, Ben," he said. He grabbed his friend's hand and then walked away, back to the Hardings' wagon.

Ben got up and brushed the dust from his pants. "My parents will be over to say goodbye in a little while," he told Sarah. "I'd better get going. They may need help packing."

Sarah grabbed Ben as he turned to leave and gave him a hug. "See you in Oregon," she said again.

40

Sarah slowly trailed back to the wagon. Jack was sitting outside with his head in his hands.

"I'm going to miss Ben," Sarah said sadly. "He never got mad at me like you do sometimes."

For once Jack didn't feel annoyed with his little sister. He knew what she said was true, and he knew how badly she felt. "I'm going to miss him, too," he told Sarah. "Ever since we left home, things seem to keep getting worse instead of better."

Sarah lifted up her chin. "When we're all in Oregon together, things will be better. I know they will." She spoke quietly, but Jack thought he saw a new light in her eyes.

Ben and his family were already gone when Jack and Sarah woke up the next morning. They both felt sad as they helped pack.

"I don't think we're going to have anything left by the time we get to Oregon," Jack grumbled as he worked. "Even our clothes and our shoes are wearing out."

"Yes, we will," Sarah said defiantly. Jack was surprised. Was this his little sister talking?

"Things will be better," she went on. "We've just got to keep going, one step at a time."

CHAPTER 6

DANGER ON THE TRAIL

After several more days the wagons finally reached Fort Bridger. Everyone had been hoping it would be a big place, so they were disappointed when all they saw were a few rough log cabins. Still, it was a place to buy supplies and rest the animals. The Hardings felt cheerful for the first time in weeks as they set up their camp.

43

Late in the afternoon, Sarah begged her mother to let her explore the area around the fort.

"I don't like the idea of your wandering off by yourself," Mrs. Harding said. "There are too many strangers around the fort."

Finally, Mr. Harding came to the rescue. He agreed to take Jack and Sarah with him while he tried to buy some supplies.

As they walked, Sarah grabbed Jack's arm. "Look," she whispered, "are those Indians?"

Jack saw a few people standing together by one of the cabins. His father had heard Sarah's question and looked, too. "Joe says those are Shoshone," he said. "They come to the fort to trade, same as we do."

The Shoshone watched as the Hardings walked by. Mr. Harding nodded his head to say hello. The Shoshone nodded back, but they didn't smile and said nothing. Jack wondered how the Shoshone people felt about all the wagon trains that were bringing so many strange, new people into the lands that had once belonged to them.

Finally, Jack, Sarah, and Mr. Harding came to a cabin with a lot of people gathered outside. Jack guessed it was a place to buy supplies. He and Sarah waited by the door while their father went inside.

When they finally got back to the wagon, Mr. Harding was grumbling as he handed his wife two small packages. "Margaret, you won't believe the prices they charge here! I couldn't buy much, but here's a bit of flour and sugar," he said.

"Well, I traded with an Indian woman while you were gone," Mrs. Harding said. She held out three pair of deerskin moccasins. "Your boots are not too worn, but the children's and my shoes are so worn we're almost barefoot. I traded the last of the sugar I had in the wagon. We can get along on that little bit you bought."

Jack and Sarah immediately took off their ragged shoes and put on the moccasins.

"You can try those new shoes out tomorrow, Jack," Mr. Harding said. "We need some fresh meat, so we'd better go hunting. Joe said there are deer in the mountains nearby."

Early the next day, Jack was ready to go hunting. He felt strange about going without Scout, but he knew his father needed help.

Just as they were ready to leave, Joe Carter asked Mr. Harding for help. He needed a few men to fix a broken wagon.

"Go on without me, Jack," Mr. Harding said. "You've gone by yourself before."

"I wasn't alone," Jack said. "Scout was always with me."

"I know it's hard," his father said. "I miss him, too. We have to think of the future though, and getting to Oregon in one piece."

Jack hung his head. "All right," he said.

Jack started walking up the path Joe had shown him. It was a beautiful day. The sky was a bright blue, and the air felt cool and fresh. As he hiked higher into the hills, he noticed a sharp pine smell from the trees on the hilltops.

Jack knew he had to be careful. Without Scout to guide him, he could easily get lost. Every few minutes he stopped and used his pocketknife to make a notch on a tree. If he got lost, he would be able to follow the notches back to camp.

Then a sudden movement in the trees just ahead made Jack stop short. He held his breath as he spied something large moving toward a clearing in the woods. Was it a deer? Jack waited.

It was a deer. Jack was sure of it. He walked carefully along the trail, trying hard to make as little noise as possible.

The deer walked into the clearing. Turning its back on Jack, it began to eat the tall grass growing underneath a large cliff that jutted out from the side of the hill.

Jack followed the deer slowly. He was kneeling down near the cliff and waiting for his chance when something made him look around. He had the strange feeling he was being watched.

Then he heard a low, growling sound. The deer heard it too and leaped away into the woods. Jack stood slowly and looked up at the edge of the cliff. He was face to face with a mountain lion.

CHAPTER 7

LOST AND FOUND

Jack froze. Don't move, he thought to himself. If I try to run, it will chase me. He realized that the mountain lion had been hunting the deer, too. Now the deer had run away, and the lion would be hungrier than ever.

Jack met the big cat's eyes, which glittered like green gems in the bright afternoon sun. Slowly, very slowly, Jack lifted his rifle, never taking his eyes off the cat. Just as slowly, the cat moved into position, ready to spring.

Suddenly the big cat leaped. Out of the corner of his eye, Jack thought he saw two animals jumping off the cliff.

In the confusion Jack shot his rifle straight up into the air. He landed on his back, trying to stay out of the cat's way. The mountain lion landed right next to him. In front of the cat was the strangest animal Jack had ever seen. It was barking furiously.

Frightened by the gunshot, the mountain lion growled and tried to swipe at the strange animal with one of its paws. When it missed, the huge cat turned and ran back into the woods.

Panting, the strange animal sat and looked at Jack. It was skinny and dirty, and along its stomach Jack could see a scar where a wound had healed. It began to whimper softly.

"It can't be," Jack said. "It can't be." He felt hot tears welling up in his eyes. "Scout!" he finally shouted. "Scout! Is it you?"

The exhausted dog walked slowly up to Jack. Slowly he lifted his head and began to lick Jack's face. Then he whined.

"Scout!" Jack shouted again. "How did you get here? Oh, Scout, I thought you were dead, and here you've saved my life!" He stared at Scout.

"Come on, boy," Jack cried, "we've got to get you something to eat and cleaned up! You're so skinny! How did you come all this way?"

Scout got slowly to his feet, and Jack picked him up. "Now I know you've lost weight, Scout," he laughed. "I could never pick you up before!"

Sarah and Jack's mother and father were working on the campfire for the evening meal when they saw Jack approach the wagon train. "What's Jack carrying?" Sarah asked as she saw her brother walking toward them.

"Well, if it's a deer, it's the smallest deer I've ever seen," Mr. Harding said.

"I think it's a dog," Sarah said as Jack got closer. "Maybe he found a hurt dog."

"That would be wonderful," said Mrs. Harding. "If he could take care of it, his pain might ease over losing Scout."

Sarah's eyes narrowed in the afternoon light. "Wait a minute. I think . . . it can't be, but I think that IS Scout!"

Sarah ran toward her brother. When Scout saw her, he struggled to get to her. He licked her face as she hugged him.

"Jack, how did you find him? How did he get here? I don't understand!" Sarah said.

"Well, I'll be. . . ." said Mr. Harding as he kneeled down. "Scout, you old rascal! You're tougher than all of us!"

Jack said nothing. He just stared happily at the ragged dog.

CHAPTER 8

JOURNEY'S END

When people in the wagon train heard about Scout, they came to hear Jack's story. Many of them brought meat and bones for the hungry dog who had traveled hundreds of miles to find his family and had fought off a mountain lion, too.

"How do you think Scout got that wound?" Jack asked his father.

"Could be he had a little disagreement with a badger or even a coyote," Mr. Harding said.

Scout sat near Jack, enjoying all the attention and his new collection of bones.

Two days after Jack found Scout, the wagon train reached a small trading post. Joe set up camp on the east side of the trading post, near a small brook. At supper that evening, he came back from the post with some bad news.

"The wagons that took the shortcut arrived here last week," he said. "They made it through, but one man was bitten by a rattlesnake and died before they left the post. Another man died along the way from drinking bad water."

Sarah and Jack looked at each other. "Do they know the names of the people who died, Mr. Carter?" Jack asked. Joe shook his head.

Sarah turned to her brother. "I'm sure it wasn't Ben. It couldn't have been," she said.

Jack was afraid to hope. He had just gotten Scout back, and he couldn't bear knowing he had now lost another good friend.

On and on the wagons traveled. Jack was tired of eating cold biscuits, bacon, and an occasional rabbit. His family had long ago used up their supply of corn and potatoes. He was tired of hearing his sister cry that her feet hurt, and he felt bad for the oxen whose heads hung lower every day.

Jack began to think about nothing more than putting one foot in front of the other. Yet no matter how tired he felt, he was always happy because Scout was back by his side once again.

Finally the wagons reached the Blue Mountains. They had gone through the desert and could now count on fresh water and grass for the animals. They were almost at the end of their journey, but they couldn't stop to rest. It was nearly mid-September, and the winter snows would soon be falling in the mountains.

One afternoon, Joe stopped the wagons early. He called everyone to a meeting.

"This is where the trail stops," he said. "Those are the Cascade Mountains up ahead, and there is no road over them." He pointed toward several tall, snow-capped peaks in the distance. "Our road now is the Columbia River. This is probably one of the most dangerous parts of the trip because we're going to have to abandon the wagons and build rafts to go down the river. Once we do that, we'll be in Oregon City and the Willamette Valley."

Many people groaned, but no one spoke. They knew they had come too far to stop now. The end of their journey was almost in sight. Everyone agreed that they would rest for a couple of days, build the rafts, then start down the river.

Two days later the wagon train awoke to a steady, cold rain. They all agreed they had to get going even in the bad weather.

Jack's father said that everyone would ride on the rafts. Because the water was so swift, the animals would have to ride on rafts, too. When he saw Jack's worried face, Mr. Harding said that Scout would stay with them.

Everyone gathered on the banks of the Columbia. Joe was already there with a group of several Indians. He explained that the Indians had traveled the river many times and would help get the rafts down to Oregon City.

The men began to load the rafts. Other men led some of the oxen onto rafts piloted by the Indians. The Hardings' raft would be one of the first to go.

Mrs. Harding and Sarah held on as the raft eased into the water. Jack held onto Scout, while Mr. Harding stood at one end, bracing the raft with the help of one of the Indians.

Suddenly the river took the raft, and they were on their way. The river was fast, but the raft floated steadily for a long way. Then the water began to swirl in a swift circle.

"Whirlpool!" Mr. Harding shouted. He began to paddle hard. The water splashed over the sides of the raft. Mrs. Harding screamed as one side tipped and Sarah toppled into the water.

Jack reached for her, but she was carried away from him. Oh, no, please! I can't lose my sister, he thought. I just can't!

Suddenly, an Indian on the raft behind them reached down into the water. He grabbed Sarah's arm and pulled her onto the raft. Sarah lay on the raft sputtering. The Hardings cried with relief. Sarah would have to make the rest of the trip on another raft, but at least she was safe.

The next day the Hardings and the other families finally came to Oregon City. Many people cheered, but then got right down to work again. Mr. Harding found a good spot to put a tent, and then he went into the center of town to check on getting some lumber to build a cabin.

When he came back, he grinned at Sarah and Jack. "I've got a surprise for you two. Look down the street," he said. When they looked they saw Ben Hamilton.

"Ben," yelled Jack, "we thought you were bitten by a rattlesnake!"

"Not yet!" laughed Ben as he ran up to the Hardings. "Your father told me you found Scout. I can't believe it!" Scout came running and jumped up on Ben.

"Where's your family? Are you near here?" Sarah asked.

"They're just down the street at the store," said Ben, as he pointed.

The three friends talked on. Jack couldn't believe it. They had made it, one step at a time, and they had found their friend. Today was the first day in their new home and the best day ever.

GLOSSARY

bracing (BRAYS ihng) making something stronger so that it will be ready for a jolt or shock

carriages (KAR ihj uz) vehicles with wheels, usually pulled by horses, that carry people

confusion (kun FYOO zhun) a mix-up or disorder

defiantly (dih FYE unt lee) a way of acting boldly and against something

exhausted (ihg ZAWS tud) very tired; weakened

jutted (JUT tud) stuck out

notch (nahch) a cut made on a surface in the form of a V

piloted (PYE lut ud) guided or steered

position (puh ZIH shun) the place where a person or thing is

reluctantly (rih LUK tunt lee) doing something in a way that shows not wanting to do it